CROCHETING IN
CIRCLES

YOU CAN ACCOMPLISH SOMETHING MARVELOUS BY CROCHETING IN CIRCLES! All ten of these amazing accessories include crocheting in rounds. The Encircled Wrap is accented by more than a dozen disc-shaped motifs, and more big dots add color to the Orange Pop Purse. Crocheting in the round also gives shape to a fashionable Josephine hat, Retro Rocket Market Bag, E-Reader Sweater, and more. Designer Sheryl Means shares her inspirations for each easy-to-intermediate pattern. We think these projects will be your all-around favorites!

TABLE OF CONTENTS

Encircled Wrap.. page 2
Bluebonnet Beret .... page 6
Running in Circles Slippers .... page 9
E-Reader Sweater .... page 12
Josephine Cloche.................................. page 14
Retro Rocket Market Bag...................... page 16
Orange Pop Purse .... page 19
Fingerless Mitts.................................... page 24
A Bushel and a Peck Scarf .... page 26
Cozy Toes Tube Slippers .... page 29
General Instructions............................. page 32
Yarn Information.................................. page 36

ABOUT SHERYL MEANS

Sheryl Means discovered her passion for crochet at an early age. "I was fascinated by yarn, color, and texture," she says, describing her introduction to the craft. "I learned to crochet as a Girl Scout. Crochet came very easily to me and I spent hours just working with yarn. When asked what I was creating, the answer was 'I don't know.' Now I see that I was a freeform crocheter in the making."

Sheryl is a Professional Member of The Crochet Guild of America and a Craft Yarn Council of America certified crochet teacher. Her designs have appeared in *Interweave Crochet* and *Crochet!* magazines. She also co-owns a yarn shop called Yarntopia in Katy, Texas. Sheryl says, "I am passionate about helping others find their creative voice."

LEISURE ARTS, INC.
Little Rock, Arkansas

ENCIRCLED WRAP

This fun shawl is worked quickly with Tunisian Stitch, then embellished with circles in four different sizes. It even has a round crocheted button to complete the circular theme.

◧■■□ INTERMEDIATE

Finished Size: Approximately 14" wide x 62" long
(35.5 cm x 157.5 cm)

MATERIALS
Medium Weight Yarn 🧶**4**
[3 ounces, 131 yards
(85 grams, 121 meters) per skein]: 3 skeins
Afghan hook, size L (8 mm) **or** size needed
for gauge
Standard crochet hook, size J (6 mm) **or** size
needed for gauge
Yarn needle

GAUGE: In Body pattern,
12 Tunisian sts and 13 rows = 4" (10 cm)
Rnds 1-3 of Large Circle = 3½" (9 cm)

Gauge Swatch: 4" (10 cm) square
Row 1: With Tunisian hook, ch 2, insert hook in second ch from hook, YO and pull up a loop, YO and draw through one loop on hook **(ch made)**, YO and draw through both loops on hook **(first fsc made)**, work 11 fsc: 12 fsc.
Rows 2-13: Work same as Body.
Finish off.

STITCH GUIDE

FOUNDATION SINGLE CROCHET
(abbreviated fsc)
Insert hook in ch at base of last fsc made, YO and pull up a loop, YO and draw through one loop on hook **(ch made)**, YO and draw through both loops on hook **(fsc made)**.
DECREASE
Pull up a loop in each of next 2 sts, YO and draw through all 3 loops on hook.

TUNISIAN CROCHET
Each row is worked in two steps. The first half is worked from **right** to **left** placing loops on the hook and the second half is worked from **left** to **right** completing each stitch. The work will not be turned unless instructed to do so and the **right** side of the work is the side facing you as you work. There will be one loop remaining on the hook at the end of each row. This is the first stitch of the next row.
TUNISIAN SIMPLE STITCH
(abbreviated Tss)
First Half: With yarn in **back** and working from **right** to **left**, skip first vertical strand, insert hook from **right** to **left** under next vertical strand **(Fig. A, page 3)**, YO and pull up a loop, continue across pulling up a loop under each vertical strand.
Second Half - row closing: Working from **left** to **right**, YO and draw through first loop on hook **(ch 1 made)**, [YO and draw through 2 loops on hook **(Fig. B, page 3)**] across until one loop remains on hook. This is the **first** stitch of the **next** row.

TUNISIAN DOUBLE CROCHET
(abbreviated Tdc)

First Half: With yarn in **back** and working from **right** to **left**, skip first vertical strand, ★ YO, insert hook from **right** to **left** under next vertical strand, YO and pull up a loop, YO and draw through 2 loops on hook *(Fig. C)*; repeat from ★ across.

Second Half - row closing: Working from **left** to **right**, YO and draw through first loop on hook **(ch 1 made)**, [YO and draw through 2 loops on hook *(Fig. B)*] across until one loop remains on hook. This is the **first** stitch of the **next** row.

Fig. A

Fig. B

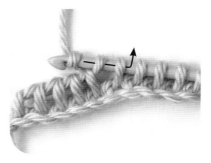

Fig. C

Row 4: Work Tdc across (40 loops on hook); close.

Repeat Rows 3 and 4 for pattern until Body measures 47" (119.5 cm), ending by working Row 4.

Last Row: Ch 1, working **between** both vertical strands **(Fig. D)**, sc in each st across; finish off.

Fig. D

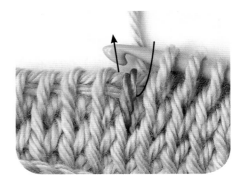

Use strandard crochet hook for all Circles and Buttons.

BODY

Row 1: With Tunisian hook, ch 2, insert hook in second ch from hook, YO and pull up a loop, YO and draw through one loop on hook **(ch made)**, YO and draw through both loops on hook **(first fsc made)**, work 38 fsc: 39 fsc.

Row 2 (Right side): **Turn**; YO, insert hook in first Fsc, YO and pull up a loop, YO and draw through 2 loops on hook, ★ YO, insert hook in next fsc, YO and pull up a loop, YO and draw through 2 loops on hook; repeat from ★ across (40 loops on hook); close.

Note: Loop a short piece of yarn around any stitch to mark Row 2 as **right** side.

Row 3: Work Tss across (40 loops on hook); close.

EXTRA LARGE CIRCLE

Rnd 1 (Right side): Ch 4, 11 dc in fourth ch from hook **(3 skipped chs count as first dc, now and throughout)**; join with slip st to first dc: 12 dc.

Note: Mark Rnd 1 as **right** side.

Rnd 2: Ch 3 **(counts as first dc, now and throughout)**, working in Back Loops Only **(Fig. 1, page 33)**, dc in same st, 2 dc in next dc and in each dc around; join with slip st to first dc: 24 dc.

Rnd 3: Ch 3, working in both loops, 2 dc in next dc, (dc in next dc, 2 dc in next dc) around; join with slip st to first dc: 36 dc.

Rnd 4: Ch 3, dc in same st and in next 2 dc, (2 dc in next dc, dc in next 2 dc) around; join with slip st to first dc: 48 dc.

Rnd 5: Ch 3, dc in same st and in next 3 dc, (2 dc in next dc, dc in next 3 dc) around; join with slip st to first dc: 60 dc.

Rnd 6: Ch 3, dc in same st and in next 4 dc, (2 dc in next dc, dc in next 4 dc) around; join with slip st to first dc, finish off leaving a long end for sewing: 72 dc.

LARGE CIRCLE (Make 4)

Rnd 1 (Right side): Ch 4, 11 dc in fourth ch from hook; join with slip st to first dc: 12 dc.

Note: Mark Rnd 1 as **right** side.

Rnd 2: Ch 3, dc in same st, 2 dc in next dc and in each dc around; join with slip st to first dc: 24 dc.

Rnd 3: Ch 3, 2 dc in next dc, (dc in next dc, 2 dc in next dc) around; join with slip st to first dc: 36 dc.

Rnd 4: Ch 3, dc in same st and in next 2 dc, (2 dc in next dc, dc in next 2 dc) around; join with slip st to first dc, finish off leaving a long end for sewing: 48 dc.

MEDIUM CIRCLE (Make 2)

Work same as Large Circle through Rnd 3; finish off leaving a long end for sewing: 36 dc.

SMALL CIRCLE (Make 4)

Work same as Large Circle through Rnd 2; finish off leaving a long end for sewing: 24 dc.

BUTTON (Make 3)

Rnd 1 (Right side): Ch 4, 11 dc in fourth ch from hook; join with slip st to first dc: 12 dc.

Note: Mark Rnd 1 as **right** side.

Rnd 2: Ch 1, working from **left** to **right**, work reverse sc in each dc around *(Figs. 6a-d, page 34)*; join with slip st to first st, finish off leaving a long end for sewing.

FINISHING

With **right** sides facing and using Diagram as a guide for placement, sew Circles to each end of Body.

DIAGRAM

EDGING

With **right** side facing and working in end of rows on Body and in sts on Circles, join yarn with sc in any st *(see Joining With Sc, page 33)*; sc evenly around working 3 sc in corners and decreasing between Circles or between Body and a Circle as needed; join with slip st to first sc, finish off.

Using Diagram as a guide, sew Buttons to Wrap. ☀

BLUEBONNET BERET

Each spring, the hills of Texas are blanketed with bluebonnets. The brilliant blue draws people from their homes out into nature. The color and stitch pattern of this hat are reminiscent of the Lone Star State's flower.

■■□□ **EASY**

Size: To fit 20" (51 cm) head measurement

MATERIALS

Medium Weight Yarn **(4)** MEDIUM
[3.5 ounces, 177 yards
(100 grams, 162 meters) per skein]: One skein
Crochet hook, size I (5.5 mm) **or** size needed
for gauge
Sewing needle and matching thread
³/₈" (10 mm) Buttons - 2

GAUGE SWATCH: 4¼" (10.75 cm) diameter
Work same as Body through Rnd 3: 24 Clusters
and 24 ch-1 sps.

STITCH GUIDE

BEGINNING CLUSTER (uses one st or sp)
Ch 2, ★ YO, insert hook in st or sp indicated,
YO and pull up a loop, YO and draw through
2 loops on hook; repeat from ★ once **more**,
YO and draw through all 3 loops on hook.
CLUSTER (uses one st or sp)
★ YO, insert hook in st or sp indicated, YO
and pull up a loop, YO and draw through
2 loops on hook; repeat from ★ 2 times **more**,
YO and draw through all 4 loops on hook.
DECREASE (uses next 2 Clusters)
† YO, insert hook in **next** Cluster, YO and
pull up a loop, YO and draw through 2 loops
on hook †, skip next ch-1 sp, repeat from
† to † once, YO and draw through all 3 loops
on hook (**counts as one dc**).
PICOT
Ch 3, slip st in third ch from hook.

BODY

Ch 5; join with slip st to form a ring.

Rnd 1 (Right side): Work beginning Cluster in
ring, ch 1, (work Cluster in ring, ch 1) 7 times;
join with slip st to top of beginning Cluster:
8 Clusters and 8 ch-1 sps.

Note: Loop a short piece of yarn around any stitch
to mark Rnd 1 as **right** side.

Rnd 2: Work beginning Cluster in same st, ch 1,
work Cluster in next ch-1 sp, ★ ch 1, work
Cluster in next Cluster, ch 1, work Cluster in next
ch-1 sp; repeat from ★ around, sc in top
of beginning Cluster to form last ch-1 sp:
16 Clusters and 16 ch-1 sps.

Rnd 3: Work (beginning Cluster, ch 1, Cluster)
in last ch-1 sp made, ch 1, work Cluster in next
ch-1 sp, ★ (work Cluster, ch 1) twice in next
ch-1 sp, work Cluster in next ch-1 sp, ch 1;
repeat from ★ around; join with slip st to top of
beginning Cluster: 24 Clusters and 24 ch-1 sps.

Rnd 4: Slip st in next ch-1 sp, work (beginning
Cluster, ch 1, Cluster) in same sp, ch 1, (work
Cluster in next ch-1 sp, ch 1) twice, ★ (work
Cluster, ch 1) twice in next ch-1 sp, (work
Cluster in next ch-1 sp, ch 1) twice; repeat from
★ around; join with slip st to top of beginning
Cluster: 32 Clusters and 32 ch-1 sps.

Rnds 5 and 6: Slip st in next ch-1 sp, work
(beginning Cluster, ch 1, Cluster) in same
sp, ch 1, skip next ch-1 sp, ★ work (Cluster,
ch 1) twice in next ch-1 sp, skip next ch-1 sp;
repeat from ★ around; join with slip st to top of
beginning Cluster.

Rnd 7: Slip st in next ch-1 sp, work (beginning Cluster, ch 1, Cluster) in same sp, ch 1, work Cluster in next ch-1 sp, ★ (work Cluster, ch 1) twice in next ch-1 sp, work Cluster in next ch-1 sp, ch 1; repeat from ★ around; join with slip st to top of beginning Cluster: 48 Clusters and 48 ch-1 sps.

Rnd 8: Slip st in next ch-1 sp, work (beginning Cluster, ch 1, Cluster) in same sp, ch 1, (work Cluster in next ch-1 sp, ch 1) twice, ★ (work Cluster, ch 1) twice in next ch-1 sp, (work Cluster in next ch-1 sp, ch 1) twice; repeat from ★ around; join with slip st to top of beginning Cluster: 64 Clusters and 64 ch-1 sps.

Rnd 9: Slip st in next ch-1 sp, work (beginning Cluster, ch 1, Cluster) in same sp, ch 1, skip next ch-1 sp, ★ (work Cluster, ch 1) twice in next ch-1 sp, skip next ch-1 sp; repeat from ★ around; join with slip st to top of beginning Cluster.

Rnd 10: Slip st in next ch-1 sp, work (beginning Cluster, ch 1, Cluster) in same sp, ★ ch 1, skip next ch-1 sp, work (Cluster, ch 1) twice in next ch-1 sp; repeat from ★ around to last ch-1 sp, skip last ch-1 sp, sc in top of beginning Cluster to form last ch-1 sp; do **not** finish off.

BAND

Row 1: Ch 3 **(counts as first dc)**, decrease, (dc in next ch-1 sp, decrease) across, dc in same sp as first dc; do **not** join: 65 dc.

Row 2: Ch 1, turn; skip first dc, sc in next dc and in each dc across, place marker in last sc made for st placement: 64 sc.

Rows 3-6: Ch 1, turn; sc in each sc across.

Finish off.

BUTTON TAB

Row 1: With **right** side facing, join yarn with sc around marked sc **(see Joining With Sc, page 33)**; sc in ends of next 4 rows on Band: 5 sc.

Rows 2-4: Ch 1, turn; sc in each sc across.

Row 5: Ch 1, turn; sc in first 2 sc, [ch 1, skip next sc **(buttonhole made)**], sc in last 2 sc: 4 sc and one ch-1 sp.

Row 6: Ch 1, turn; sc in first 2 sc and in next ch-1 sp, sc in last 2 sc: 5 sc.

Rows 7 and 8: Ch 1, turn; sc in each sc across.

Rows 9 and 10: Repeat Rows 5 and 6; do **not** finish off.

EDGING

Ch 1, turn; sc in first 4 sc, 2 sc in last sc; working in ends of rows on Button Tab, skip first row, sc in next 9 rows; working in sc on Band, (sc in next 4 sc, work Picot) across to last 4 sc, sc in next 3 sc, 2 sc in last sc; working in ends of rows on Band, skip first row, sc in next 4 rows, 3 sc in last row; sc in last ch-1 sp on Rnd 10 of Body; 3 sc in end of Row 1 on Band, sc in end of each row across, sc in same st as first sc; join with slip st to first sc, finish off.

Sew buttons to Band opposite buttonholes. ◉

RUNNING IN CIRCLES SLIPPERS

Bright colorful slippers will make everyone's feet happy.   Make a pair for each member of the family!

◼◼☐☐ **EASY**

Size	Finished Foot Length and Circumference
X-Small	7" x 5³/₄" (18 cm x 14.5 cm)
Small	8¹/₄" x 7" (21 cm x 18 cm)
Medium	10" x 8¹/₂" (25.5 cm x 21.5 cm)
Large	11" x 10" (28 cm x 25.5 cm)
X-Large	11¹/₂" x 11¹/₄" (29 cm x 28.5 cm)

Size Note: Instructions are written with sizes X-Small and Small in the first set of braces { } and sizes Medium, Large, and X-Large in the second set of braces. Instructions will be easier to read if you circle all the numbers pertaining to your size. If only one number is given, it applies to all sizes.

MATERIALS
Medium Weight Yarn 🧶**4** MEDIUM
   [3.5 ounces, 177 yards
   (100 grams, 162 meters) per skein]:
      Pink, Blue **and** Green - One skein
      each color
Crochet hook, size G (4 mm) **or** size
   needed for gauge

GAUGE: 17 sc and 20 rnds = 4" (10 cm)

Gauge Swatch: 1³/₄" (4.5 cm) diameter
Work same as Toe through Rnd 4: 24 sc.

TOE

Rnd 1 (Right side)**:** With Pink, ch 2, 6 sc in second ch from hook; join with slip st to first sc.

Note: Loop a short piece of yarn around any stitch to mark Rnd 1 as **right** side.

Rnd 2: Ch 1, 2 sc in same st and in each sc around; join with slip st to first sc: 12 sc.

Rnd 3: Ch 1, 2 sc in same st, sc in next sc, (2 sc in next sc, sc in next sc) around; join with slip st to first sc: 18 sc.

Rnd 4: Ch 1, 2 sc in same st, sc in next 2 sc, (2 sc in next sc, sc in next 2 sc) around; join with slip st to first sc: 24 sc.

Size X-Small ONLY
Rnds 5-8: Ch 1, sc in same st and in each sc around; join with slip st to first sc.

Finish off.

Size Small ONLY
Rnd 5: Ch 1, 2 sc in same st, sc in next 3 sc, (2 sc in next sc, sc in next 3 sc) around; join with slip st to first sc: 30 sc.

Rnds 6-8: Ch 1, sc in same st and in each sc around; join with slip st to first sc.

Finish off.

Size Medium ONLY
Rnd 5: Ch 1, 2 sc in same st, sc in next 3 sc, (2 sc in next sc, sc in next 3 sc) around; join with slip st to first sc: 30 sc.

Rnd 6: Ch 1, 2 sc in same st, sc in next 4 sc, (2 sc in next sc, sc in next 4 sc) around; join with slip st to first sc: 36 sc.

Rnds 7 and 8: Ch 1, sc in same st and in each sc around; join with slip st to first sc.

Finish off.

Size Large and X-Large ONLY
Rnd 5: Ch 1, 2 sc in same st, sc in next 3 sc, (2 sc in next sc, sc in next 3 sc) around; join with slip st to first sc: 30 sc.

Rnd 6: Ch 1, 2 sc in same st, sc in next 4 sc, (2 sc in next sc, sc in next 4 sc) around; join with slip st to first sc: 36 sc.

Rnd 7: Ch 1, 2 sc in same st, sc in next 5 sc, (2 sc in next sc, sc in next 5 sc) around; join with slip st to first sc: 42 sc.

Size Large ONLY
Rnd 8: Ch 1, sc in same st and in each sc around; join with slip st to first sc, finish off.

Size X-Large ONLY
Rnd 8: Ch 1, 2 sc in same st, sc in next 6 sc, (2 sc in next sc, sc in next 6 sc) around; join with slip st to first sc, finish off: 48 sc.

FOOT - ALL SIZES

Rnd 1: With **right** side facing, join Blue with sc in first sc *(see Joining With Sc, page 33)*; sc in next sc and in each sc around; join with slip st to first sc.

Rnd 2: Ch 1, sc in same st and in each sc around; join with slip st to first sc.

Rnd 3: Ch 1, sc in same st and in each sc around; join with slip st to first sc changing to Green *(Fig. 4, page 34)*.

STRIPE SEQUENCE
★ One rnd/row Green, 3 rnds/rows Blue, 4 rnds/rows Pink, 3 rnds/rows Blue; repeat from ★ throughout Foot and Heel.

Following Stripe Sequence and changing color in same manner, repeat Rnd 2 for pattern until Foot measures {4-5¼}{6¾-7¾-8¾}"/{10-13.5} {17-19.5-22} cm.

Increase Rnd: Ch 1, sc in same st and in each sc around to last sc, 2 sc in last sc: {25-31} {37-43-49} sc.

Finish off. Place marker in {6th-8th}{10th-11th-13th}-to-the-last sc for st placement.

HEEL

Row 1: With **right** side facing, join next color yarn with sc in marked sc; do **not** remove marker, sc in next {12-16}{20-22-26} sc, leave remaining {12-14}{16-20-22} sts unworked: {13-17} {21-23-27} sc.

Row 2: Ch 1, turn; sc in each sc across.

To change colors at the end of a row, work the last sc to within one step of completion, hook new yarn and draw through both loops on hook.

Repeat Row 2 until Heel measures approximately {2¼-2}{2¼-2¼-1¾}"/{5.5-5}{5.5-5.5-4.5} cm.

Finish off.

BACK

Row 1: With **right** side facing, join next color with sc in first sc; sc in next {3-5}{7-8-10} sc, decrease, sc in next sc, decrease, sc in last {4-6}{8-9-11} sc: {11-15}{19-21-25} sc.

Row 2: Ch 1, turn; sc in first {3-5}{7-8-10} sc, decrease, sc in next sc, decrease, sc in last {3-5}{7-8-10} sc: {9-13}{17-19-23} sc.

Sizes Small, Medium, Large, and X-Large ONLY
Row 3: Ch 1, turn; sc in first {4}{6-7-9} sc, decrease, sc in next sc, decrease, sc in last {4}{6-7-9} sc: {11}{15-17-21} sc.

Row 4: Ch 1, turn; sc in first {3}{5-6-8} sc, decrease, sc in next sc, decrease, sc in last {3}{5-6-8} sc: {9}{13-15-19} sc.

ALL SIZES
Fold Heel Back with **right** side together and matching sts.

Joining: Ch 1, with **wrong** side facing and working through both layers, slip st through inside loops of sc across; finish off.

SIDES

Row 1: With **right** side facing, join same color yarn as last rnd of Foot with slip st in marked sc, remove marker; ch 1, sc in end of each row across Heel and Heel Back, slip st in same st on last rnd of Foot as Row 1 of Heel.

Row 2: Ch 1, turn; skip first slip st, sc in each sc across, skip last slip st and slip st in next sc on last rnd of Foot.

Row 3: Ch 1, turn; skip first slip st, sc in each sc across, skip last slip st and slip st in next sc on last rnd of Foot; finish off.

Begin working in rounds.

Rnd 1: With **right** side facing, skip first 4 sc on Sides and join next color with sc in next sc; sc in each sc across to center back (above seam), decrease, sc in each sc across to last sc on Sides, sc in last sc, place marker around sc just made; sc in each sc across last rnd of Foot working in same sc as slip sts, sc in first sc on Row 3, place marker around sc just made, sc in last 3 sc; join with slip st to first sc.

Rnd 2: Ch 1, ★ sc in each sc around to next marked sc, skip marked sc, sc in next sc, move marker to sc just made; repeat from ★ once **more**, sc in last 2 sc; join with slip st to first sc.

Rnd 3: Ch 1, ★ sc in each sc around to next marked sc, skip marked sc, sc in next sc, remove marker; repeat from ★ once **more**, sc in last sc; join with slip st to first sc, finish off.

TRIM

With **right** side facing, join next color with slip st in any sc; ch 1, working from **left** to **right**, work reverse sc in each sc around *(Figs. 6a-d, page 34)*; join with slip st to first st, finish off. ☼

E-READER SWEATER

Protect your e-reader and look stylish at the same time! The Body is worked in the round then embellished with circles. Choose your favorite colors or go for the purple!

◼◼☐☐ **EASY**

Finished Size: 5" wide x 7½" tall
(12.5 cm x 19 cm)

MATERIALS

Medium Weight Yarn 🧶**4**
[3.5 ounces, 155 yards
(100 grams, 142 meters) per skein]:
Violet - One skein
Purple - Small amount
Crochet hooks, sizes H (5 mm), I (5.5 mm),
and J (6 mm) **or** sizes needed for gauge
Yarn needle

GAUGE: With largest size hook,
14 hdc and 9 rows = 4" (10 cm)

Gauge Swatch: 4" (10 cm) square
Row 1: With largest size hook and Violet,
ch 3, YO, insert hook in third ch from hook
(2 skipped chs count as first hdc), YO and pull
up a loop, YO and draw through one loop on hook
(ch made), YO and draw through all 3 loops on
hook **(first fhdc made)**, work 13 fhdc: 14 fhdc.
Rows 2-9: Ch 2 **(counts as first hdc)**, turn; hdc in
next st and in each st across.
Finish off.

BODY

Rnd 1: With largest size hook and Violet,
ch 3, YO, insert hook in third ch from hook
**(2 skipped chs count as first hdc, now and
throughout)**, YO and pull up a loop, YO and
draw through one loop on hook **(ch made)**, YO
and draw through all 3 loops on hook **(first fhdc
made)**, work 34 fhdc; being careful not to twist
rnd, join with slip st to first hdc: 36 sts.

Rnd 2 (Right side)**:** Ch 2 **(counts as first hdc, now
and throughout)**, turn; working in Front Loops
Only **(Fig. 1, page 33)**, hdc in next fhdc and in
each fhdc around; join with slip st to first hdc.

Note: Loop a short piece of yarn around any stitch
to mark Rnd 2 as **right** side.

Rnd 3: Ch 2, turn; working in Back Loops Only, hdc in next hdc and in each hdc around; join with slip st to first hdc.

Rnd 4: Ch 2, turn; working in Front Loops Only, hdc in next hdc and in each hdc around; join with slip st to first hdc.

Rnds 5-12: Repeat Rnds 3 and 4, 4 times.

Change to medium size hook.

Rnd 13: Ch 1, do **not** turn; working in both loops, sc in same st and in each hdc around; join with slip st to first sc.

Rnds 14-16: Ch 1, sc in same st and in each sc around; join with slip st to first sc.

Finish off, leaving a long end for sewing.

RIBBING

Rnd 1: With **right** side facing, working in chs at base of sts on Row 1, and using larger size hook, join Violet with dc in first ch *(see Joining With Dc, page 33)*; dc in next ch and in each ch around; join with slip st to first dc: 36 dc.

Rnd 2: Slip st from **back** to **front** around post of same st, ch 3 **(counts as first BPdc, now and throughout)**, work FPdc around next dc, (work BPdc around next dc, work FPdc around next dc) around; join with slip st to first BPdc.

Rnd 3: Slip st from **back** to **front** around post of same st, ch 3, work FPdc around next FPdc, (work BPdc around next BPdc, work FPdc around next FPdc) around; join with slip st to first BPdc, finish off.

TRIM
FIRST CIRCLE
Rnd 1 (Right side): With smaller size hook and Purple, ch 3, 8 hdc in third ch from hook; join with slip st to first hdc, finish off: 9 hdc.

Note: Mark Rnd 1 as **right** side.

SECOND THRU EIGHTH CIRCLES
Rnd 1 (Right side): With smaller size hook and Purple, ch 3, 8 hdc in third ch from hook; with **right** side of **previous Circle** facing, slip st in fifth hdc; join with slip st to first hdc on **new Circle**, finish off.

FINISHING
Fold Body with joining at center. Thread yarn needle with long end. With **wrong** side together, whipstitch bottom closed *(Fig. 5, page 34)*.

Sew Trim to Body below Ribbing. ☀

JOSEPHINE CLOCHE

The cloche is associated with flappers and the fashion of the 1920s. Bobbed haircuts, jazz music, and an outspoken lifestyle are all part of the flapper image. Singer Josephine Baker embodied these qualities, and it is for her I named this hat.

◼◼■☐☐ EASY

Size: To fit a 22" (56 cm) head measurement

MATERIALS
Medium Weight Yarn **[4]**
  [3.5 ounces, 155 yards
  (100 grams, 142 meters) per skein]:
    Navy **and** Violet - One skein **each** color
Crochet hook, size I (5.5 mm) **or** size needed
  for gauge
Yarn needle
Brooch (optional)

GAUGE SWATCH: 4" (10 cm)
Work same as Body through Rnd 7: 42 sc.

STITCH GUIDE
DECREASE (uses next 2 hdc)
★ YO, insert hook in **next** hdc, YO and pull up a loop; repeat from ★ once **more**, YO and draw through all 5 loops on hook **(counts as one hdc)**.

BODY
Rnd 1 (Right side): With Navy, ch 2, 6 sc in second ch from hook; do **not** join, place marker to mark beginning of rnd **(see Markers, page 33)**.

Note: Loop a short piece of yarn around any stitch to mark Rnd 1 as **right** side.

Work in Back Loops Only throughout Body **(Fig. 1, page 33)**.

Rnd 2: 2 Sc in each sc around: 12 sc.

Rnd 3: (2 Sc in next sc, sc in next sc) around: 18 sc.

Rnd 4: (2 Sc in next sc, sc in next 2 sc) around: 24 sc.

Rnd 5: (2 Sc in next sc, sc in next 3 sc) around: 30 sc.

Rnd 6: (2 Sc in next sc, sc in next 4 sc) around: 36 sc.

Rnd 7: (2 Sc in next sc, sc in next 5 sc) around: 42 sc.

Rnd 8: (2 Sc in next sc, sc in next 6 sc) around: 48 sc.

Rnd 9: (2 Sc in next sc, sc in next 7 sc) around: 54 sc.

Rnd 10: (2 Sc in next sc, sc in next 8 sc) around: 60 sc.

Rnd 11: (2 Hdc in next sc, hdc in next 9 sc) around: 66 hdc.

Rnd 12: (2 Hdc in next hdc, hdc in next 10 hdc) around: 72 hdc.

Rnd 13: (2 Hdc in next hdc, hdc in next 11 hdc) around: 78 hdc.

Rnds 14-16: Hdc in each hdc around.

Rnd 17: Hdc in next 18 hdc, place marker around last hdc made for st placement, decrease, (hdc in next 17 hdc, decrease) 3 times, hdc in next hdc; slip st in next hdc, finish off: 74 hdc.

BRIM

Rnd 1: With **right** side facing and working in both loops, join Violet with dc in same hdc as last slip st made *(see Joining With Dc, page 33)*, dc in next hdc and in each hdc around; join with slip st to first dc.

Rnd 2: Ch 3 **(counts as first dc, now and throughout)**, ★ skip next dc, dc in next dc, working **around** dc just made, dc in skipped dc; repeat from ★ around to last dc, skip last dc, dc in same st as first dc, working **around** dc just made, dc in skipped dc; join with slip st to first dc: 75 dc.

Rnd 3: Ch 3, dc in next dc and in each dc around; join with slip st to first dc.

Rnd 4: Ch 1, sc in same st and in next 9 dc, (sc, hdc) in next dc, hdc in next 54 dc, sc in last 10 dc; join with slip st to first sc: 76 sts.

Rnd 5: Ch 1, sc in same st and in next 15 sts, hdc in next 45 hdc, sc in last 15 sts; join with slip st to first sc.

Rnd 6: Ch 1, sc in same st and in next 14 sc, hdc in next 45 sts, sc in last 16 sts; join with slip st to first sc, finish off.

Rnd 7: With **right** side facing, join Navy with slip st in any st; working from **left** to **right**, work reverse sc in each st around *(Figs. 6a-d, page 34)*; join with slip st to first st, finish off.

BAND

Row 1: With **right** side facing and working toward Brim, join Navy with sc around marked hdc; sc around same st, 2 sc around dc on next rnd: 4 sc.

Row 2: Ch 3, turn; 3 dc in first sc, skip next 2 sc, sc in last sc: 5 sts.

Row 3: Ch 3, turn; 3 dc in first sc, skip next 2 dc, sc in next dc, leave last dc unworked.

Repeat Row 3 for pattern until Band measures approximately 22" (56 cm) long **or** one more row than length to fit around Hat; finish off.

Wrap Band around Hat and overlap Row 1. Tack in place and pin with a brooch if desired. ☀

RETRO ROCKET MARKET BAG

Who doesn't have fond memories of tasty treats from the ice cream man? These colors reminded me of rocket-shaped ice cream pops. I just had to use those hues in a swirling bag for summer days filled with shopping.

 EASY

Finished Size (after felting): Approximately 10" diameter x 13" tall (25.5 cm x 33 cm)(excluding Handles)

MATERIALS
100% Wool Medium Weight Yarn **(4)**
[3.5 ounces, 155 yards
(100 grams, 142 meters) per skein]:
    Red, Blue, **and** White - One skein **each** color
Crochet hook, size J (6 mm) **or** size
    needed for gauge
Yarn needle
1¹/₂" (4 cm) D rings - 4

GAUGE SWATCH: 4¹/₂" (11.5 cm) diameter
Work same as Body through Rnd 3: 45 dc.

STITCH GUIDE
DECREASE (uses next 2 sts)
Pull up a loop in each of next 2 sts, YO and draw through all 3 loops on hook **(counts as one sc)**.

BODY
With Red, ch 6; join with slip st to form a ring.

Rnd 1 (Right side)**:** Ch 3 **(counts as first dc, now and throughout)**, 14 dc in ring; join with slip st to first dc: 15 dc.

Note: Loop a short piece of yarn around any stitch to mark Rnd 1 as **right** side.

Rnd 2: Ch 3, dc in same st, 2 dc in next dc and in each dc around; join with slip st to first dc: 30 dc.

Rnd 3: Ch 3, 2 dc in next dc, (dc in next dc, 2 dc in next dc) around; join with slip st to first dc: 45 dc.

Rnd 4: Ch 3, dc in next dc, 2 dc in next dc, (dc in next 2 dc, 2 dc in next dc) around; join with slip st to first dc: 60 dc.

Rnd 5: Ch 3, dc in next 2 dc, 2 dc in next dc, (dc in next 3 dc, 2 dc in next dc) around; join with slip st to first dc: 75 dc.

Rnd 6: Ch 3, dc in next 3 dc, 2 dc in next dc, (dc in next 4 dc, 2 dc in next dc) around; join with slip st to first dc: 90 dc.

Rnd 7: Ch 3, dc in next 2 dc, ch 2, skip next 2 dc, ★ dc in next 3 dc, ch 2, skip next 2 dc; repeat from ★ around; join with slip st to first dc: 54 dc and 18 ch-2 sps.

Rnd 8: Slip st in next dc, ch 3, dc in next dc, 2 dc in next ch-2 sp, ch 2, skip next dc, ★ dc in next 2 dc, 2 dc in next ch-2 sp, ch 2, skip next dc; repeat from ★ around; join with slip st to first dc, finish off: 72 dc and 18 ch-2 sps.

Rnd 9: With **right** side facing, join Blue with dc in third dc of any 4-dc group *(see Joining With Dc, page 33)*; dc in next dc, 2 dc in next ch-2 sp, ch 2, skip next 2 dc, ★ dc in next 2 dc, 2 dc in next ch-2 sp, ch 2, skip next 2 dc; repeat from ★ around; join with slip st to first dc.

Rnd 10: Slip st in next 2 dc, ch 3, dc in next dc, 2 dc in next ch-2 sp, ch 2, skip next 2 dc, ★ dc in next 2 dc, 2 dc in next ch-2 sp, ch 2, skip next 2 dc; repeat from ★ around; join with slip st to first dc, finish off.

Rnd 11: With White, repeat Rnd 9.

Rnds 12 and 13: Slip st in next 2 dc, ch 3, dc in next dc, 2 dc in next ch-2 sp, ch 2, skip next 2 dc, ★ dc in next 2 dc, 2 dc in next ch-2 sp, ch 2, skip next 2 dc; repeat from ★ around; join with slip st to first dc.

Finish off.

Rnds 14 and 15: Repeat Rnds 9 and 10.

Rnd 16: With Red, repeat Rnd 9.

Rnds 17-20: Slip st in next 2 dc, ch 3, dc in next dc, 2 dc in next ch-2 sp, ch 2, skip next 2 dc, ★ dc in next 2 dc, 2 dc in next ch-2 sp, ch 2, skip next 2 dc; repeat from ★ around; join with slip st to first dc.

Finish off.

Rnd 21: With **right** side facing, join Blue with dc in third dc of any 4-dc group; dc in next dc, 2 dc in next ch-2 sp, ch 2, skip next 2 dc, ★ dc in next 2 dc, 2 dc in next ch-2 sp, ch 2, skip next 2 dc; repeat from ★ around; join with slip st to first dc, finish off.

Rnd 22: With White, repeat Rnd 21.

Rnd 23: Repeat Rnd 21.

Rnd 24: With **right** side facing, join Red with dc in third dc of any 4-dc group; dc in next dc, 2 dc in next ch-2 sp, ch 1, skip next 2 dc, ★ dc in next 2 dc, 2 dc in next ch-2 sp, ch 1, skip next 2 dc; repeat from ★ around; join with slip st to first dc, do **not** finish off: 72 dc and 18 ch-1 sps.

Rnd 25: Slip st in next 2 dc, ch 3, dc in next dc, 2 dc in next ch-1 sp, skip next 2 dc, ★ dc in next 2 dc, 2 dc in next ch-1 sp, skip next 2 dc; repeat from ★ around; join with slip st to first dc: 72 dc.

Rnd 26: Ch 1, sc in same st and in next dc, decrease, (sc in next 2 dc, decrease) around; join with slip st to first sc: 54 sc.

Rnd 27: Ch 1, sc in same st, † working **around** D ring, sc in next 5 sc, sc in next 8 sc †, working **around** D ring, sc in next 5 sc, sc in next 9 sc, repeat from † to † twice; join with slip st to first sc, finish off.

HANDLE (Make 2 - one **each** Red and Blue)
Ch 4; join with slip st to form a ring.

Rnd 1: Ch 1, 4 sc in ring; do **not** join, place marker to mark beginning of rnd **(see Markers, page 33)**.

Rnd 2: Sc in each sc around.

Repeat Rnd 2 for pattern until Handle measures approximately 42" (106.5 cm).

Finish off.

FINISHING
Felt Bag and Handles **(see Felting Basics, page 35)**. This bag should be lightly felted with some stitch definition remaining.

Thread Red Handle through 2 D rings on same side of bag, then thread Blue Handle through rings on opposite side. Thread yarn needle with either color and sew each end of Red Handle to Blue Handle forming a circle.

HANDLE WRAP (Make 2)
With 2 strands of White held together, ch 21.

Row 1 (Right side)**:** Sc in second ch from hook and in each ch across: 20 sc.

Note: Mark Row 1 as **right** side.

Rows 2-6: Ch 1, turn; sc in each sc across.

Joining Row: Ch 1, turn; place Wrap around Handle at seam and working in free loops of beginning ch **(Fig. 2, page 33)** and in sts on Row 6, sc in each st across; finish off. ☀

ORANGE POP PURSE

I am a child of the 1970s. This bright and funky felted bag will make you want to do the hustle!

▮▮▮▯▯ **EASY**

Shown on page 21.

Finished Size: 11" tall x 11" wide
(28 cm x 28 cm) (after felting,
excluding Gusset and Handles)

MATERIALS

100% Wool Medium Weight Yarn
    [3.5 ounces, 155 yards
    (100 grams, 142 meters) per skein]:
        Orange - 4 skeins
        Blue, Purple, **and** Violet - One skein
            each color
Crochet hook, size I (5.5 mm) **or** size needed
    for gauge
Yarn needle
2" (5 cm) diameter Metal rings - 8

GAUGE SWATCH: 4" (10 cm) diameter
Work same as Body through Rnd 3: 36 dc.

STITCH GUIDE

HALF DOUBLE DECREASE
    (abbreviated hdc decrease) (uses next 2 sts)
★ YO, insert hook in **next** st, YO and pull up
a loop; repeat from ★ once **more**, YO and
draw through all 5 loops on hook **(counts as
one hdc)**.
DOUBLE CROCHET DECREASE
    (abbreviated dc decrease) (uses next 2 dc)
★ YO, insert hook in **next** dc, YO and pull
up a loop, YO and draw through 2 loops on
hook; repeat from ★ once **more**, YO and
draw through all 3 loops on hook **(counts as
one dc)**.

BODY (Make 2)

Rnd 1 (Right side): With Orange, ch 4, 11 dc
in fourth ch from hook **(3 skipped chs count
as first dc, now and throughout)**: join with
slip st to first dc: 12 dc.

Note: Loop a short piece of yarn around any
stitch to mark Rnd 1 as **right** side.

Rnd 2: Ch 3 **(counts as first dc, now and
throughout)**, dc in same st, 2 dc in next dc
and in each dc around; join with slip st to
first dc: 24 dc.

Rnd 3: Ch 3, dc in same st and in next dc,
(2 dc in next dc, dc in next dc) around; join
with slip st to first dc: 36 dc.

Rnd 4: Ch 3, dc in same st and in next 2 dc,
(2 dc in next dc, dc in next 2 dc) around;
join with slip st to first dc: 48 dc.

Rnd 5: Ch 3, dc in same st and in next 3 dc,
(2 dc in next dc, dc in next 3 dc) around;
join with slip st to first dc: 60 dc.

Rnd 6: Ch 3, dc in same st and in next 4 dc,
(2 dc in next dc, dc in next 4 dc) around;
join with slip st to first dc: 72 dc.

Rnd 7: Ch 3, dc in same st and in next 5 dc,
(2 dc in next dc, dc in next 5 dc) around;
join with slip st to first dc: 84 dc.

Rnd 8: Ch 3, dc in same st and in next 6 dc,
(2 dc in next dc, dc in next 6 dc) around;
join with slip st to first dc: 96 dc.

Rnd 9: Ch 3, dc in same st and in next 7 dc, (2 dc in next dc, dc in next 7 dc) around; join with slip st to first dc: 108 dc.

Rnd 10: Ch 3, dc in same st and in next 8 dc, (2 dc in next dc, dc in next 8 dc) around; join with slip st to first dc: 120 dc.

Rnd 11: Ch 3, dc in same st and in next 9 dc, (2 dc in next dc, dc in next 9 dc) around; join with slip st to first dc: 132 dc.

Rnd 12: Ch 3, dc in same st and in next 10 dc, (2 dc in next dc, dc in next 10 dc) around; join with slip st to first dc: 144 dc.

Rnd 13: Ch 3, dc in same st and in next 11 dc, (2 dc in next dc, dc in next 11 dc) around; join with slip st to first dc, do **not** finish off: 156 dc.

GUSSET

Row 1: Ch 3, **turn**; working Back Loops Only **(Fig. 1, page 33)**, dc in next 128 dc, leave remaining 27 dc unworked: 129 dc.

Row 2: Ch 3, turn; dc in next dc and in each dc across.

Row 3: Ch 3, turn; working in Back Loops Only, dc in next dc and in each dc across; finish off.

With **wrong** sides together and Orange, whipstitch Body together **(Fig. 5, page 34)**.

TAB

Row 1: With **right** side facing, join Orange with slip st in last unworked dc **before** Gusset on either side of Body; ch 2, working in ends of rows on Gusset, 2 dc in first row, 3 dc in each of next 4 rows, dc in last row, YO, insert hook in last row, YO and pull up a loop, YO and draw through 2 loops on hook, YO, insert hook in next dc on Body, YO and pull up a loop, YO and draw through 2 loops on hook, YO and draw through all 3 loops on hook **(counts as one dc):** 16 dc.

Rows 2-4: Ch 2, turn; dc in next dc and in each dc across to last 2 dc, dc decrease, leave beginning ch-2 unworked: 10 dc.

Rows 5-15: Ch 3, turn; dc in next dc and in each dc across.

Finish off, leaving a long end for sewing.

Thread yarn needle with long end. Fold ends of rows on Tab to **wrong** side, then sew them together down to Row 7. Insert end of Tab through one ring and sew Tab in place. Continue to sew ends of rows together down to Row 3, then secure end.

Repeat on opposite side of Body.

CIRCLES
X-SMALL (Make 9 **total** - 3 Orange/Violet, 2 **each** Orange/Blue and Orange/Purple, one Blue/Purple and one Violet/Blue)

Rnd 1 (Right side)**:** With first color yarn indicated, ch 2, 6 sc in second ch from hook; join with slip st to first sc changing to next color yarn **(Fig. 4, page 34)**.

Note: Mark Rnd 1 as **right** side.

Rnd 2: Ch 1, 2 sc in same st and in each sc around; join with slip st to first sc, finish off leaving a long end for sewing: 12 sc.

SMALL (Make 2 - one **each** Blue/Violet and Violet/Blue)
Rnd 1 (Right side)**:** With first color yarn indicated, ch 4, 11 dc in fourth ch from hook; join with slip st to first dc changing to next color yarn: 12 dc.

Note: Mark Rnd 1 as **right** side.

Rnd 2: Ch 1, 2 sc in same st as joining and in each dc around; join with slip st to first sc, finish off leaving a long end for sewing: 24 sc.

FIRST MEDIUM CIRCLE (Make one)
Rnd 1 (Right side)**:** With Purple, ch 4, 11 dc in fourth ch from hook; join with slip st to first dc: 12 dc.

Note: Mark Rnd 1 as **right** side.

Rnd 2: Ch 3, dc in same st, 2 dc in next dc and in each dc around; join with slip st to first dc changing to Blue: 24 dc.

Rnd 3: Ch 3, dc in same st and in next dc, (2 dc in next dc, dc in next dc) around; join with slip st to first dc changing to Violet: 36 dc.

Rnd 4: Ch 1, 2 sc in same st, sc in next 2 dc, (2 sc in next dc, sc in next 2 dc) around; join with slip st to first sc, finish off leaving a long end for sewing: 48 sc.

SECOND MEDIUM CIRCLE (Make one)
Rnd 1 (Right side): With Orange, ch 4, 11 dc in fourth ch from hook; join with slip st to first dc changing to Blue: 12 dc.

Note: Mark Rnd 1 as **right** side.

Rnd 2: Ch 3, dc in same st, 2 dc in next dc and in each dc around; join with slip st to first dc: 24 dc.

Rnd 3: Ch 3, dc in same st and in next dc, (2 dc in next dc, dc in next dc) around; join with slip st to first dc changing to Purple: 36 dc.

Rnd 4: Ch 3, dc in same st and in next 2 dc, (2 dc in next dc, dc in next 2 dc) around; join with slip st to first dc, finish off leaving a long end for sewing: 48 dc.

THIRD MEDIUM CIRCLE (Make one)
Rnd 1 (Right side): With Blue, ch 4, 11 dc in fourth ch from hook; join with slip st to first dc: 12 dc.

Note: Mark Rnd 1 as right side.

Rnd 2: Ch 3, dc in same st, 2 dc in next dc and in each dc around; join with slip st to first dc changing to Orange: 24 dc.

Rnd 3: Ch 3, dc in same st and in next dc, (2 dc in next dc, dc in next dc) around; join with slip st to first dc changing to Violet: 36 dc.

Rnd 4: Ch 3, dc in same st and in next 2 dc, (2 dc in next dc, dc in next 2 dc) around; join with slip st to first dc changing to Blue: 48 dc.

Rnd 5: Ch 1, 2 sc in same st, sc in next 3 dc, (2 sc in next dc, sc in next 3 dc) around; join with slip st to first sc, finish off leaving a long end for sewing: 60 sc.

FOURTH MEDIUM CIRCLE (Make one)
Rnd 1 (Right side)**:** With Violet, ch 4, 11 dc in fourth ch from hook; join with slip st to first dc changing to Purple: 12 dc.

Note: Mark Rnd 1 as **right** side.

Rnd 2: Ch 3, dc in same st, 2 dc in next dc and in each dc around; join with slip st to first dc changing to Blue: 24 dc.

Rnd 3: Ch 3, dc in same st and in next dc, (2 dc in next dc, dc in next dc) around; join with slip st to first dc changing to Purple: 36 dc.

Rnd 4: Ch 3, dc in same st and in next 2 dc, (2 dc in next dc, dc in next 2 dc) around; join with slip st to first dc, finish off leaving a long end for sewing: 48 dc.

LARGE (Make 2 - one **each** Blue/Violet/Purple/Orange/Blue and Violet/Purple/Orange/Blue/Violet)
Rnd 1: With first color yarn indicated, ch 4, 11 dc in fourth ch from hook; join with slip st to first dc: 12 dc.

Note: Mark Rnd 1 as **right** side.

Rnd 2: Ch 3, dc in same st, 2 dc in next dc and in each dc around; join with slip st to first dc changing to next color yarn: 24 dc.

Rnd 3: Ch 3, dc in same st and in next dc, (2 dc in next dc, dc in next dc) around; join with slip st to first dc changing to next color yarn: 36 dc.

Rnd 4: Ch 1, 2 sc in same st, sc in next 2 dc, (2 sc in next dc, sc in next 2 dc) around; join with slip st to first sc changing to next color yarn: 48 sc.

Rnd 5: Ch 1, 2 sc in same st, sc in next 3 sc, (2 sc in next sc, sc in next 3 sc) around; join with slip st to first sc changing to next color yarn: 60 sc.

Rnd 6: Ch 1, 2 sc in same st, sc in next 4 sc, (2 sc in next sc, sc in next 4 sc) around; join with slip st to first sc, finish off leaving a long end for sewing: 72 sc.

BUTTON (Make 2 - one **each** Purple/Blue/Orange and Blue/Purple/Orange)
Rnd 1 (Right side)**:** With first color yarn indicated, ch 4, 11 dc in fourth ch from hook; join with slip st to first dc changing to next color yarn: 12 dc.

Note: Mark Rnd 1 as **right** side.

Rnd 2: Ch 1, 2 sc in same st and in each dc around; join with slip st to first sc changing to next color yarn: 24 sc.

Rnd 3: Ch 2 (**counts as first hdc**), hdc in next sc and in each sc around; join with slip st to first hdc.

Rnd 4: Ch 1, beginning in first hdc, hdc decrease around; join with slip st to first hdc, finish off leaving a long end for sewing: 12 hdc.

Thread yarn needle with long end. Weave needle through hdc on Rnd 4. Before closing, stuff Button with yarn scraps, then gather **tightly** and secure end.

FROG CLOSURE

Rnd 1: With Blue, ch 2, 3 sc in second ch from hook; do **not** join, place marker to mark beginning of rnd **(see Markers, page 33)**.

Rnd 2: Working in Back Loops Only, sc in each sc around.

Repeat Rnd 2 until piece measures approximately 18" (45.5 cm) long; finish off leaving a long end for sewing.

Thread yarn needle with long end and sew last rnd to first rnd forming a circle. Sew circle around one Button, crossing remainder of circle close to Button to form a figure 8.

Sew Frog Closure to top edge of Body and sew remaining Button to opposite top edge.

HANDLE
FIRST SECTION

Row 1: With Orange, work 10 sc around metal ring on either Tab.

Rows 2-14: Ch 2 **(counts as first hdc)**, turn; hdc in next st and in each st across.

Finish off, leaving a long end for sewing.

Thread yarn needle with long end and sew last row around another metal ring.

NEXT 5 SECTIONS

Row 1: With Orange, work 10 sc around same metal ring as last Section was sewn to.

Rows 2-14: Ch 2 **(counts as first hdc)**, turn; hdc in next st and in each st across.

Finish off, leaving a long end for sewing.

Thread yarn needle with long end and sew last row around another metal ring.

LAST SECTION

Work same as Next 5 Sections, sewing last row of Last Section around metal ring attached to Tab on opposite side, being careful not to twist Handle.

FINISHING

Using photos as a guide, sew all circles in place.

Felt the Purse **(see Felting Basics, page 35)**.

Front

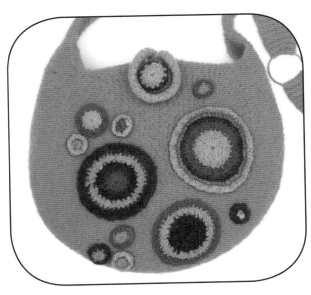

Back

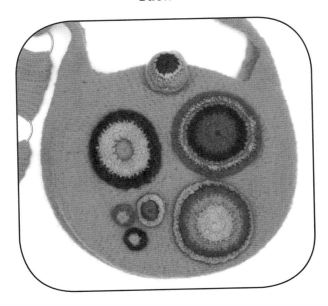

FINGERLESS MITTS

Bulky enough to add a little warmth but lacy enough to be feminine, these mitts make great gifts!

Finished Size: 8½" circumference x 8" high
(21.5 cm x 20.5 cm)

MATERIALS
Medium Weight Yarn
[3.5 ounces, 177 yards
(100 grams, 162 meters) per skein]: One skein
Crochet hook, size I (5.5 mm) **or** size needed
for gauge

GAUGE SWATCH: 8½" circumference x 3" high
(21.5 cm x 7.5 cm)
Work same as Mitt through Rnd 5: 10 Cross Sts.

STITCH GUIDE

FOUNDATION DOUBLE CROCHET *(abbreviated fdc)*
YO, insert hook in ch at base of last fdc made, YO and
pull up a loop, YO and draw through one loop on hook
(ch made), (YO and draw through 2 loops on hook)
twice **(fdc made)**.

BACK POST DOUBLE CROCHET *(abbreviated BPdc)*
YO, insert hook from **back** to **front** around post of st
indicated *(Fig. 3, page 33)*, YO and pull up a loop
(3 loops on hook), (YO and draw through 2 loops on
hook) twice.

FRONT POST DOUBLE CROCHET *(abbreviated FPdc)*
YO, insert hook from **front** to **back** around post of st
indicated *(Fig. 3, page 33)*, YO and pull up a loop
(3 loops on hook), (YO and draw through 2 loops on
hook) twice.

CROSS STITCH *(abbreviated Cross St)* (uses next 3 sts)
Skip next st, dc in next 2 sts, working **around** 2 dc just
made, dc in skipped st.

MITT (Make 2)

Rnd 1 (Right side): Ch 4, YO, insert
hook in fourth ch from hook **(3 skipped
chs count as first dc)**, YO and pull up a
loop, YO and draw through one loop on
hook **(ch made)**, (YO and draw through
2 loops on hook) twice **(first fdc made)**,
work 28 fdc; join with slip st to first
dc: 30 sts.

Rnd 2: Slip st from **back** to **front**
around post of same st, ch 3 **(counts
as first BPdc)**, work FPdc around next
fdc, (work BPdc around next fdc, work
FPdc around next fdc) around; join
with slip st to first BPdc.

Rnd 3: Slip st in next FPdc, ch 3
**(counts as first dc, now and
throughout)**, dc in next st, working
around 2 dc just made, dc in same st
as joining slip st **(first Cross St made)**,
work Cross Sts around; join with slip st
to first st: 10 Cross Sts.

Rnds 4-7: Slip st in next dc, ch 3, dc
in next dc, working **around** 2 dc just
made, dc in same st as joining slip st
**(counts as first Cross St, now and
throughout)**, work Cross St around; join
with slip st to first dc.

Rnd 8: Slip st in next dc, ch 3, dc
in next dc, working **around** 2 dc just
made, dc in same st as joining slip st,
work Cross Sts around to last 3 sts,
skip next dc, dc in next dc, skip last
dc; join with slip st to first dc: 9 Cross
Sts and one dc.

Rnd 9: Slip st in next dc, ch 3, dc in next dc, working **around** 2 dc just made, dc in last dc on Rnd 8, work 8 Cross Sts; join with slip st to first dc: 9 Cross Sts.

Rnd 10: Slip st in next dc, ch 3, dc in next dc, working **around** 2 dc just made, dc in same st as joining slip st, work 7 Cross Sts, sc in same dc as second dc made on last Cross St and in last 3 dc; join with slip st to first dc: 28 sts.

Rnd 11: Slip st in next dc, ch 3, dc in next dc, working **around** 2 dc just made, dc in same st as joining slip st, work 7 Cross Sts, ch 2, skip last 4 sc; join with slip st to first dc: 24 dc and 2 chs.

Rnd 12: Slip st in next dc, ch 3, dc in next dc, working **around** 2 dc just made, dc in same st as joining slip st, work 7 Cross Sts, dc in next 2 chs, working **around** 2 dc just made, dc in same dc as second dc made on last Cross St; join with slip st to first dc: 9 Cross Sts.

Rnds 13 and 14: Slip st in next dc, ch 3, dc in next dc, working **around** 2 dc just made, dc in same st as joining slip st, work Cross Sts around; join with slip st to first dc.

Rnd 15: Ch 1, sc in same st and in each st around; join with slip st to first sc, finish off. ☀

A BUSHEL AND A PECK SCARF

When my granddaughters were toddlers, I used to sing "I love you a bushel and a peck, with a hug around the neck." These little red circles remind me of special moments with loved ones.

◀◼◻◻◻ **EASY +**

Finished Size: 6" wide x 70" long
(15 cm x 178 cm)

MATERIALS
Medium Weight Yarn **4** MEDIUM
[3.5 ounces, 177 yards
(100 grams, 162 meters) per skein]:
2 skeins
Crochet hook, size H (5 mm) **or** size needed
for gauge
Yarn needle

GAUGE SWATCH: 3" (7.5 cm) diameter
Work same as Medium Circle: 15 Clusters and 15
ch-1 sps.

STITCH GUIDE

2-DC CLUSTER (uses one st)
★ YO, insert hook in st indicated, YO and pull
up a loop, YO and draw through 2 loops on
hook; repeat from ★ once **more**, YO and draw
through all 3 loops on hook.
3-DC CLUSTER (uses one st)
★ YO, insert hook in st indicated, YO and pull
up a loop, YO and draw through 2 loopson
hook; repeat from ★ 2 times **more**, YO and
draw through all 3 loops on hook.

MEDIUM CIRCLE (Make 14)
Ch 5; join with slip st to form a ring.

Rnd 1 (Right side): Ch 3 (**counts as first dc, now
and throughout**), 14 dc in ring; join with slip st to
first dc: 15 dc.

Note: Loop a short piece of yarn around any stitch
to mark Rnd 1 as **right** side.

Rnd 2: Ch 3, work 2-dc Cluster in same st as
joining, ch 1, (work 3-dc Cluster in next dc,
ch 1) around; join with slip st to top of first 2-dc
Cluster, finish off: 15 Clusters and 15 ch-1 sps.

LARGE CIRCLE (Make 14)
Ch 5; join with slip st to form a ring.

Rnd 1 (Right side): Ch 3, 17 dc in ring; join with
slip st to first dc: 18 dc.

Note: Mark Rnd 1 as **right** side.

Rnd 2: Ch 1, sc in same st, ch 4, skip next 2 dc,
★ sc in next dc, ch 4, skip next 2 dc; repeat from
★ around; join with slip st to first sc: 6 ch-4 sps.

Rnd 3: Slip st in next ch-4 sp, ch 3, 5 dc in same sp, 6 dc in next ch-4 sp and in each ch-4 sp around; join with slip st to first dc, finish off: six 6-dc groups.

SMALL CIRCLE (Make 6)
Ch 5; join with slip st to form a ring.

Rnd 1 (Right side): Ch 3, 17 dc in ring; join with slip st to first dc, finish off: 18 dc.

Note: Mark Rnd 1 as **right** side.

ASSEMBLY
STRIP (Make 2)
FIRST 2 CIRCLES JOINING
With **right** side facing, join yarn with slip st in any ch-1 sp on any Medium Circle, ch 4; with **right** side of any Large Circle facing, slip st in first dc of any 6-dc group and in next 3 dc, ch 4; with **right** side of joined Medium Circle facing, slip st in second ch-1 sp **before** previous slip st; finish off.

NEXT MEDIUM CIRCLE JOINING

With **right** side of previous Large Circle facing, skip next two 6-dc groups from last joining slip st and join yarn with slip st in sixth dc of **next** 6-dc group, ch 4; with **right** side of new Medium Circle facing, slip st in any ch-1 sp, (slip st in next Cluster and in next ch-1 sp) twice; ch 4, with **right** side of joined Large Circle facing, join with slip st to first dc of same 6-dc group as first joining slip st; finish off.

NEXT LARGE CIRCLE JOINING

With **right** side of previous Medium Circle facing, skip next 7 ch-1 sps from last joining slip st and join yarn with slip st in next ch-1 sp, ch 4; with **right** side of new Large Circle facing, slip st in first dc of any 6-dc group and in next 3 dc, ch 4; with **right** side of joined Medium Circle facing, slip st in second ch-1 sp **before** previous slip st; finish off.

Repeat Next Medium Circle Joining and Next Large Circle Joining, 5 times for a total of 14 Circles joined.

EDGING

With **right** side of one Strip facing, join yarn with sc in any st **(see Joining With Sc, page 33)**; ch 1, (sc in next st, ch 1) around working 4 sc in each ch-4 sp and one sc in each ch-1 sp; join with slip st to first sc, finish off.

Place Strips together with first Medium Circle of one Strip between last Large and Medium Circles of remaining Strip. With **wrong** sides together and working in inside loops of sc on Edging, whipstitch Strips together **(Fig. 5, page 34)**.

FRINGE (Make 6)

Ch 20; with **right** side facing, slip st in any dc on Small Circle, **turn**; 2 sc in next ch and in each ch across to last 3 chs, sc in last 3 chs; finish off leaving a long end for sewing.

At each end of Scarf, sew 2 Fringes to each Large Circle and one Fringe to each Medium Circle. ✺

COZY TOES TUBE SLIPPERS

Make your feet cozy and happy while wearing these comfy slippers. They feel great and can be a warm way to use up small amounts of yarn. Follow this striping pattern or make up your own!

◖■◗□□ **EASY**

Finished Size: 11" long x 8½" circumference
(28 cm x 21.5 cm)

MATERIALS
Medium Weight Yarn ⑷
[3.5 ounces, 177 yards
(100 grams, 162 meters) per skein]:
Red, Green, Yellow, **and** Purple -
One skein **each** color
Crochet hooks, sizes H (5 mm) **and** I (5.5 mm)
or sizes needed for gauge

GAUGE: In pattern, 15 dc = 4" (10 cm)

Gauge Swatch: 2" (5 cm) diameter
Work through Rnd 5 of Toe.

STITCH GUIDE

DECREASE
Pull up a loop in each of next 2 sts, YO and draw through all 3 loops on hook **(counts as one sc)**.

BACK POST DOUBLE CROCHET
(abbreviated BPdc)
YO, insert hook from **back** to **front** around post of st indicated **(Fig. 3, page 33)**, YO and pull up a loop (3 loops on hook), (YO and draw through 2 loops on hook) twice.

FRONT POST DOUBLE CROCHET
(abbreviated FPdc)
YO, insert hook from **front** to **back** around post of st indicated **(Fig. 3, page 33)**, YO and pull up a loop (3 loops on hook), (YO and draw through 2 loops on hook) twice.

TOE

Rnd 1 (Right side)**:** With smaller size hook and Red, ch 2, 6 sc in second ch from hook; join with slip st to first sc.

Note: Loop a short piece of yarn around any stitch to mark Rnd 1 as **right** side.

Rnd 2: Ch 1, 2 sc in same st and in each sc around; join with slip st to first sc: 12 sc.

Rnd 3: Ch 1, 2 sc in same st, sc in next sc, (2 sc in next sc, sc in next sc) around; join with slip st to first sc: 18 sc.

Rnd 4: Ch 1, 2 sc in same st, sc in next 2 sc, (2 sc in next sc, sc in next 2 sc) around; join with slip st to first sc: 24 sc.

Rnd 5: Ch 1, 2 sc in same st, sc in next 3 sc, (2 sc in next sc, sc in next 3 sc) around; join with slip st to first sc: 30 sc.

Rnds 6 and 7: Ch 1, sc in same st and in each sc around; join with slip st to first sc.

Finish off.

FOOT

Rnd 1: With **right** side facing and using larger size hook, join Green with dc in any sc **(see Joining With Dc, page 33)**; dc in next sc and in each sc around; join with slip st to first dc.

Rnd 2: Ch 2, dc in same st and in each dc around; cut Green, skip beginning ch-2 and join with slip st to first dc changing to Yellow **(Fig. 4, page 34)**.

Change colors in same manner throughout.

Rnd 3: Ch 1, sc in same st and in each dc around; join with slip st to first sc changing to Purple.

Rnd 4: Ch 2, dc in same st and in each sc around; skip beginning ch-2 and join with slip st to first dc.

Rnd 5: Ch 2, dc in same st and in each dc around; skip beginning ch-2 and join with slip st to first dc changing to Yellow.

Rnd 6: Ch 1, sc in same st and in each dc around; join with slip st to first sc changing to Green.

Rnd 7: Ch 1, sc in same st and in each sc around; join with slip st to first sc changing to Purple.

Rnd 8: Ch 2, dc in same st and in each sc around; skip beginning ch-2 and join with slip st to first dc changing to Yellow.

Rnd 9: Ch 1, sc in same st and in each dc around; join with slip st to first sc changing to Green.

Rnd 10: Ch 1, sc in same st and in each sc around; join with slip st to first sc changing to Red.

Rnds 11-13: Ch 1, sc in same st and in each sc around; join with slip st to first sc.

Rnd 14: Ch 1, sc in same st and in each sc around; join with slip st to first sc changing to Green.

Rnds 15 and 16: Repeat Rnds 4 and 5.

Rnd 17: Ch 1, sc in same st and in each dc around; join with slip st to first sc changing to Purple.

Rnds 18 and 19: Repeat Rnds 4 and 5.

Rnd 20: Ch 1, sc in same st and in next 12 dc, decrease, sc in next dc and in each dc around to last 2 dc, decrease; join with slip st to first sc changing to Green: 28 sc.

Rnd 21: Ch 1, sc in same st and in each sc around; join with slip st to first sc changing to Purple.

Rnd 22: Ch 2, dc in same st and in each sc around; skip beginning ch-2 and join with slip st to first dc changing to Yellow.

Rnd 23: Ch 1, sc in same st and in each dc around; join with slip st to first sc changing to Green.

Rnd 24: Ch 1, sc in same st and in next 11 sc, decrease, sc in each sc around to last 2 sc, decrease; join with slip st to first sc changing to Red: 26 sc.

CUFF

Rnd 1: With smaller size hook, ch 2, dc in same st and in each sc around; skip beginning ch-2 and join with slip st to first dc.

Rnd 2: Ch 2, work FPdc around same st, work BPdc around next dc, (work FPdc around next dc, work BPdc around next dc) around; skip beginning ch-2 and join with slip st to first FPdc.

Rnd 3: Ch 2, work FPdc around same st, work BPdc around next BPdc, (work FPdc around next FPdc, work BPdc around next BPdc) around; skip beginning ch-2 and join with slip st to first FPdc, finish off. ✸

GENERAL INSTRUCTIONS

ABBREVIATIONS

BPdc	Back Post double crochet(s)
ch(s)	chain(s)
cm	centimeters
dc	double crochet(s)
fdc	foundation double crochet(s)
fhdc	foundation half double crochet(s)
FPdc	Front Post double crochet(s)
fsc	foundation single crochet(s)
hdc	half double crochet(s)
mm	millimeters
Rnd(s)	Round(s)
sc	single crochet(s)
sp(s)	space(s)
st(s)	stitch(es)
Tdc	Tunisian double crochet(s)
Tss	Tunisian simple stitch(es)
YO	yarn over

★ — work instructions following ★ as **many more** times as indicated in addition to the first time.

† to † — work all instructions from first † to second † **as many** times as specified.

( ) or [ ] — work enclosed instructions **as many** times as specified by the number immediately following **or** work all enclosed instructions in the stitch or space indicated **or** contains explanatory remarks.

colon (:) — the number(s) given after a colon at the end of a row or round denote(s) the number of stitches or spaces you should have on that row or round.

CROCHET HOOKS

Metric mm	U.S.
2.25	B-1
2.75	C-2
3.25	D-3
3.5	E-4
3.75	F-5
4	G-6
5	H-8
5.5	I-9
6	J-10
6.5	K-10½
8	L-11
9	M/N-13
10	N/P-15
15	P/Q
16	Q
19	S

CROCHET TERMINOLOGY

UNITED STATES		INTERNATIONAL
slip stitch (slip st)	=	single crochet (sc)
single crochet (sc)	=	double crochet (dc)
half double crochet (hdc)	=	half treble crochet (htr)
double crochet (dc)	=	treble crochet(tr)
treble crochet (tr)	=	double treble crochet (dtr)
double treble crochet (dtr)	=	triple treble crochet (ttr)
triple treble crochet (tr tr)	=	quadruple treble crochet (qtr)
skip	=	miss

▮▯▯▯ BEGINNER	Projects for first-time crocheters using basic stitches. Minimal shaping.
▮▮▯▯ EASY	Projects using yarn with basic stitches, repetitive stitch patterns, simple color changes, and simple shaping and finishing.
▮▮▮▯ INTERMEDIATE	Projects using a variety of techniques, such as basic lace patterns or color patterns, mid-level shaping and finishing.
▮▮▮▮ EXPERIENCED	Projects with intricate stitch patterns, techniques and dimension, such as non-repeating patterns, multi-color techniques, fine threads, small hooks, detailed shaping and refined finishing.

GAUGE

Exact gauge is **essential** for proper size. Before beginning your project, make the sample swatch given in the individual instructions in the yarn and hook specified. After completing the swatch, measure it carefully. If your swatch is larger or smaller than specified, **make another, changing hook size to get the correct gauge.** Keep trying until you find the size hook that will give you the specified gauge.

MARKERS

Markers are used to help distinguish the beginning of each round being worked. Place a 2" (5 cm) scrap piece of yarn before the first stitch of each round, moving marker after each round is complete.

JOINING WITH SC

When instructed to join with sc, begin with a slip knot on hook. Insert hook in stitch or space indicated, YO and pull up a loop, YO and draw through both loops on hook.

JOINING WITH DC

When instructed to join with dc, begin with a slip knot on hook. YO, holding loop on hook, insert hook in stitch or space indicated, YO and pull up a loop (3 loops on hook), (YO and draw through 2 loops on hook) twice.

BACK OR FRONT LOOP ONLY

Work only in loop(s) indicated by arrow *(Fig. 1)*.

Fig. 1

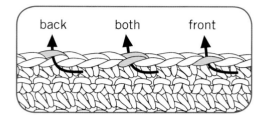

FREE LOOPS OF A CHAIN

When instructed to work in free loops of a chain, work in loop indicated by arrow *(Fig. 2)*.

Fig. 2

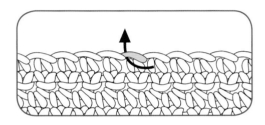

POST STITCH

Work around post of stitch indicated, inserting hook in direction of arrow *(Fig. 3)*.

Fig. 3

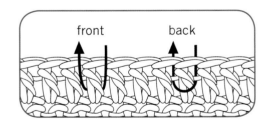

Yarn Weight Symbol & Names	LACE 0	SUPER FINE 1	FINE 2	LIGHT 3	MEDIUM 4	BULKY 5	SUPER BULKY 6
Type of Yarns in Category	Fingering, 10-count crochet thread	Sock, Fingering Baby	Sport, Baby	DK, Light Worsted	Worsted, Afghan, Aran	Chunky, Craft, Rug	Bulky, Roving
Crochet Gauge* Ranges in Single Crochet to 4" (10 cm)	32-42 double crochets**	21-32 sts	16-20 sts	12-17 sts	11-14 sts	8-11 sts	5-9 sts
Advised Hook Size Range	Steel*** 6,7,8 Regular hook B-1	B-1 to E-4	E-4 to 7	7 to I-9	I-9 to K-10.5	K-10.5 to M-13	M-13 and larger

*GUIDELINES ONLY: The chart above reflects the most commonly used gauges and hook sizes for specific yarn categories.

** Lace weight yarns are usually crocheted on larger-size hooks to create lacy openwork patterns. Accordingly, a gauge range is difficult to determine. Always follow the gauge stated in your pattern.

*** Steel crochet hooks are sized differently from regular hooks–the higher the number the smaller the hook, which is the reverse of regular hook sizing.

CHANGING COLORS

To join with a slip stitch with new color yarn, cut old yarn, insert hook in stitch indicated, YO with new yarn *(Fig. 4)* and draw through stitch **and** loop on hook.

Fig. 4

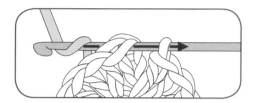

WHIPSTITCH

Place two pieces with **wrong** sides together. Sew through both pieces once to secure the beginning of the seam, leaving an ample yarn end to weave in later. Insert the needle from **front** to **back** through **inside** loop only of each stitch on **both** pieces *(Fig. 5)*. Bring the needle around and insert it from **front** to **back** through next loop of both pieces. Continue in this manner across, keeping the sewing yarn fairly loose.

Fig. 5

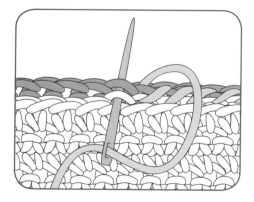

REVERSE SINGLE CROCHET
(abbreviated reverse sc)

Working from **left** to **right**, ★ insert hook in stitch to **right** of hook *(Fig. 6a)*, YO and draw through, under and to left of loop on hook (2 loops on hook) *(Fig. 6b)*, YO and draw through both loops on hook *(Fig. 6c)* **(reverse sc made, *Fig. 6d)*;** repeat from ★ around.

Fig. 6a

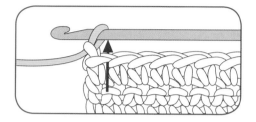

Fig. 6b

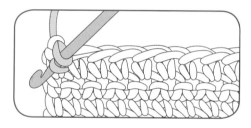

Fig. 6c

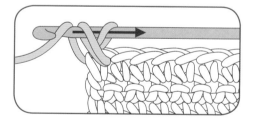

Fig. 6d

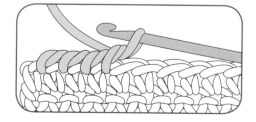

FELTING BASICS

Felting is simple, just 4 easy steps. All you are really doing is shrinking and changing the texture of your crocheted project.

1. START WITH WONDERFUL WOOL YARN

Read the label. AVOID "superwash" wool or wool yarns labeled as machine washable as they are made specifically to NOT shrink. We used 100% wool to make the Orange Pop Purse and the Retro Rocket Market Bag, so in order to have yours turn out close to the same size, look on the label for wool content.

2. CROCHET THE PROJECT

Make a test swatch to felt before starting the project. Make the swatch to test your gauge, make sure the yarn felts the way you want it, and make sure that your colors don't run.

3. MACHINE FELT THE PROJECT

Set your top-loading washing machine for a HOT wash and a COLD rinse cycle. Add about a tablespoon of detergent to the wash. Place your project in a tight-mesh lingerie or sweater bag and toss it into the machine. Throw in an old pair of jeans to speed up the felting process (the more agitation, the better). Check every 2-3 minutes during the wash cycle to keep an eye on size and shrinkage of your project. A properly felted project has shrunk to the desired size and the stitches are hard to see. When checking, you may want to wear rubber gloves to protect your hands from the hot water. Once it's felted, remove it from the machine and allow the water to spin out. Put the project back in for the cold rinse.

4. BLOCK THE PROJECT

Roll the project in a towel and gently squeeze out the excess water. Don't wring the towel as that may set in permanent creases. Gently stretch and shape the project by stuffing it with paper towels. Let the piece air dry. This may take several days, depending on the weather.

YARN INFORMATION

Each project in this leaflet was made using Medium Weight Yarn. Any brand of Medium Weight Yarn may be used. It is best to refer to the yardage/meters when determining how many balls or skeins to purchase. Remember, to arrive at the finished size, it is the GAUGE/TENSION that is important, not the brand of yarn. For your convenience, listed below are the specific yarns used to create our photography models.

ENCIRCLED WRAP
Stitch Nation by Debbie Stroller™ Alpaca Love™
#3580 Dusk

BLUEBONNET BERET
Stitch Nation by Debbie Stroller™ Bamboo Ewe™
#5830 Periwinkle

RUNNING IN CIRCLES SLIPPERS
Stitch Nation by Debbie Stroller™ Bamboo Ewe™
Pink - #5705 Snapdragon
Blue - #5510 Beach Glass
Green - #5625 Sprout

E-READER SWEATER
Stitch Nation by Debbie Stroller™ Full O' Sheep™
Violet - #2925 Passionfruit
Purple - #2550 Plummy

JOSEPHINE CLOCHE
Stitch Nation by Debbie Stroller™ Full O' Sheep™
Navy - #2820 Ocean
Violet - #2925 Passionfruit

RETRO ROCKET MARKET BAG
Stitch Nation by Debbie Stroller™ Full O' Sheep™
Red - #2910 Poppy
Blue - #2510 Aquamarine
White - #2205 Little Lamb

ORANGE POP PURSE
Stitch Nation by Debbie Stroller™ Full O' Sheep™
Orange - #2260 Clementine
Blue - #2510 Aquamarine
Purple - #2550 Plummy
Violet - #2925 Passionfruit

FINGERLESS MITTS
Stitch Nation by Debbie Stroller™ Bamboo Ewe™
#5410 Mercury

A BUSHEL AND A PECK SCARF
Stitch Nation by Debbie Stroller™ Bamboo Ewe™
#5910 Lipstick

COZY TOES TUBE SLIPPERS
Stitch Nation by Debbie Stroller™ Bamboo Ewe™
Red - #5910 Lipstick
Green - #5625 Sprout
Yellow - #5230 Buttercup
Purple - #5560 Grape

We have made every effort to ensure that these instructions are accurate and complete. We cannot, however, be responsible for human error, typographical mistakes, or variations in individual work.

PRODUCTION TEAM
Instructional Writer/Editor - Sarah J. Green; Editorial Writer - Susan McManus Johnson; Senior Graphic Artist - Lora Puls; Graphic Artist - Becca Snider; Photography Manager - Katherine Laughlin; Photo Stylist - Angela Alexander; and Photographer - Jason Masters.